# *Fish* ON THE *Move*

## The Story of the Striped Bass Migration

JEREMY PALLAI

Illustrated by JEAN LEARY PALLAI

BLUEFISH RIVER PRESS

Born in freshwater rivers and flows,
baby striped bass live life on the go.

They race over currents, rock piles and pools,
swimming in packs referred to as schools.

While rivers are where they spend childhood days,
their journey soon leads to the ocean and bays.

Feasting on clams, baitfish and crustaceans,
they'll eat almost anything—no reservations!

As spring arrives and the water is warming,
stripers take notice and then they start swarming.

For they prefer water that isn't too hot—
somewhere near 60 degrees hits the spot.

To find cooler waters they begin their migration
up the coast to the north—a summer vacation!

From the Outer Banks and Chesapeake Bay,
to Long Island Sound they make their way.

On to Cape Cod like an underwater train,
some even swim as far north as Maine.

But in a few months when the leaves start to turn,
it gets too cold in the north, and then they return.

Back to their roots and the rivers of birth,
full from the feedings, bigger in girth.

It's happened like this as long as we know,
up and down the east coast, the ebb and the flow.

**For Wyatt, Zach, and Fiona—**
May their generation protect the world's fisheries.

Jeremy Pallai / Bluefish River Press

Bluefish River Press
455 Washington Street, Box 194
Duxbury, MA 02331

www.fishonthemove.info

Illustration © 2015, Jean Leary Pallai
Editing, Megan Pallai

Boston / Jeremy M. Pallai — First Edition
ISBN 978-0971470170